·CAIRNGORM AND SPEYSIDE·

COLIN BAXTER

RICHARD DREW PUBLISHING
GLASGOW

SUNRISE OVER
ABERNETHY FOREST

OVERLEAF:
CRAIGGOWRIE AND
THE CAIRNGORMS

WIDE CONTRASTS IN THE SCENERY OF SCOTLAND ALWAYS IMPRESS THE VISITOR. WHERE ELSE CAN BE FOUND IN SO SMALL AN AREA MOUNTAINS, SAVAGE SEAS, ROUGH COASTS, WOODED VALLEYS, WILD MOORLAND, TUMBLING RIVERS AND FERTILE PLAINS? CHANGING PLAY OF LIGHT BROUGHT BY THE FICKLE CLIMATE ADDS MYSTERY TO THE SCOTTISH EXPERIENCE.

NO-ONE IN RECENT YEARS HAS CAPTURED THIS EVER-CHANGING VARIETY AS SENSITIVELY AS THE PHOTOGRAPHER, COLIN BAXTER, WHO HAS IN THIS SERIES SELECTED CERTAIN AREAS AND THEMES TO CONVEY THE RICH DIVERSITY OF SCOTLAND'S CITIES AND COUNTRYSIDE.

ALTHOUGH THE UPPER SPEY VALLEY IS ONE OF THE FEW INLAND AREAS OF THE HIGHLANDS, WATER IS NEVER FAR AWAY. THE SPEY ITSELF WIDENS INTO LOCH INSH AND LOCH MORLICH IS A TRUE MOUNTAIN LAKE, BUT MOUNTAINS DOMINATE WITH SOME OF BRITAIN'S HIGHEST IN THE CAIRNGORM RANGE. THEIR DEVELOP-MENT, ESPECIALLY FOR SKI-ING IN THE LAST THIRTY YEARS, HAS MEANT THE ENCROACHMENT OF VISIBLE TOURISM; YET THE WILDERNESS IS ALWAYS CLOSE AT HAND, WHETHER IN THE CALEDONIAN PINES OF THE FOREST OF ROTHIEMURCHUS OR ON THE HIGH PLATEAU OF THE CAIRNGORMS.

Carn Eilrig

Loch an Eilein

RIVER SPEY
AND GLEN FESHIE

BRAERIACH,
CREAG DHUBH
AND LOCH AN EILEIN

Loch Pityoulish

LOCH ALVIE

SCOTS PINES

ROTHIEMURCHUS AND
THE CAIRNGORMS

CREAG DHUBH

LOCH INSH AND
THE SPEY VALLEY

INSHRIACH FOREST

CARN EILRIG
FROM LOCH MORLICH

HEATHER BURNING

Loch an Eilein

OVERLEAF:
Spey Valley

FACING PAGE:
Loch Morlich
and Rothiemurchus

Stones
in Loch Morlich

Loch an Eilein

Loch Gamhna

NEAR INSH

FLOOD
IN SPEY VALLEY

BOAT OF GARTEN

CREAG A' CHALAMAIN

ROTHIEMURCHUS
AND SPEY VALLEY

MONADHLIATH
MOUNTAINS
AND SPEY VALLEY

CREAG LOISGTE,
GLEN MORE
FOREST PARK

LOCH MORLICH
IN WINTER

COIRE CAS
AND LOCH MORLICH

ORD BAN
AND CREAG DHUBH

First Published 1986 by
RICHARD DREW PUBLISHING
6 CLAIRMONT GARDENS, GLASGOW, G3 7LW, SCOTLAND

Printed and bound in Great Britain by
Blantyre Printing and Binding Co. Ltd.

British Library Cataloguing in Publication Data

"Cairngorm and Speyside — (Experience Scotland)
1. Moray (Grampian) — Description and
travel — Guide-books 2. Spey, River,
Valley (Scotland) — Description and
travel — Guide-books 3. Cairngorms
(Scotland) — Description and travel —
Guide-books
I. Title   II. Series
914.12'23   DA880.M8

ISBN 0-86267-156-6